SCHIRMER PERFORMANCE EDITIONS

LABORUM DULCE LENIMEN

G. SCHIRMER

HAL LEONARD PIANO LIBRARY

SCHUBERT
FOUR IMPROMPTUS
D. 899 (Opus 90)

Edited and Recorded by Immanuela Gruenberg

T0210310

To access companion recorded performances online, visit:
www.halleonard.com/mylibrary

Enter Code
2532-8133-9708-6140

On the cover:
A Schubert Evening in a Vienna Salon
by Julius Schmid
(1854–1935)
© The Bridgeman Art Library

ISBN 978-1-4234-3112-1

G. SCHIRMER, Inc.

DISTRIBUTED BY
HAL•LEONARD®
CORPORATION
7777 W. BLUEMOUND RD. P.O. BOX 13819 MILWAUKEE, WI 53213

www.musicsalesclassical.com
www.halleonard.com

CONTENTS

HISTORICAL NOTES

Franz Schubert (1797–1828)

Of all the great composers associated with Vienna, Franz Schubert was the only one born in the city. Schubert's father was a schoolmaster and a good enough violinist to teach the boy the instrument. The eldest brother Ignaz taught Franz piano. By the age of ten the young Schubert had also studied organ, harmony, and singing with the organist of the Catholic church in the district where the family lived.

In 1808 Franz, whose extraordinary musical talents were evident, was accepted a choirboy at the imperial court chapel, which also included admission to the Imperial and Royal City College, a boarding school. Here Schubert's musical education gained more sophistication. Schubert began composing at least as early as age twelve; by the age of sixteen he had written numerous string quartets, songs, German dances, and other pieces. Antonio Salieri, court composer at Vienna, noticed the talented boy and instructed him personally in composition until 1816.

Under pressure from his father, Schubert trained to become a school teacher and began teaching at his father's school in the autumn of 1814. He continued in that capacity for two years, though unhappy teaching school, as it distracted him from composition.

For most of his life Schubert struggled financially as a freelance composer in Vienna, seeking commissions and public performances, unsuccessfully attempting to gain court appointments, and making small incomes from publishers. He often relied on the help of patrons and close friends who were as devoted to him as he was to them. His circle of followers gathered for evenings called Schubertiads, where the composer's songs, piano music, and chamber compositions were performed in private homes.

The composer suffered from ill health in the last years of his life. Schubert's death at age thirty-one on November 19, 1828, was likely from syphilis. His many close friends raised money for a monument to him, erected in 1830, with the following inscription: "The art of music here entombed a rich possession, but even fairer hopes."

Schubert aspired to fame in the large forms of opera and the symphony in the model of Beethoven, but fell short of his hopes. Nevertheless, Schubert was far from unknown in his lifetime. His music was reviewed and discussed often in the press, particularly in his last two years. Schubert composed an enormous amount of music in his brief life: operas, incidental theatre music, choral works, symphonies and overtures, chamber music, extensive piano music, and over 600 songs (lieder). Schubert's achievements in lieder were unique and paramount, creating a body of song fully exploring the lyric possibilities of romantic German poetry.

Schubert is important as one of the major masters of the nineteenth century, especially as a transitional figure from the Classical to the Romantic age. He clung to Classical forms, but infused them with a fresh sense of harmony and melody. In the decades after his death Schubert was known as a master lieder composer, but his reputation as an instrumental and orchestral composer took longer to build, not reaching full esteem until the twentieth century.

Schubert's publishers often asked for short piano pieces of moderate difficulty. The Four Impromptus, D. 899 (Op. 90), may have been in response to such a request. They were probably composed in the summer and/or autumn of 1827, one of the happiest times in Schubert's life, marked by travel with friends and a particularly pleasant stay in Graz in September. The Impromptus and the *Moments musicaux* were in the tradition (possibly at a publisher's suggestion) of similar works by Václav Jan Křtitel Tomášek (1774–1850), a Bohemian composer known for short piano works of romantic lyricism, though Schubert's compositions are completely original in style and content.

Other compositions of the summer and autumn of 1827 include the Piano Trio in E-flat Major, the Fantasy in C Major for piano and violin, the *Deutsche Messe*, some small choral works, *12 Grazer Walzer* (piano), *Kindermarsch* for piano duet, and various lieder. Schubert composed another set of Four Impromptus, D. 935 (Op. 142), in December of 1827.

Schubert was a diminutive man in stature, less than five feet in height. His poor vision required eye glasses, shown in all drawings of him. By most accounts he was a likable man of good humor, though sometimes irritable due to illness, or dreamy and distracted by composition. An anecdote shows something of Schubert's somewhat humble personality. Ludwig van Beethoven (1770–1827) was the towering musical figure in Vienna during Schubert's lifetime. Schubert held him in high regard, but the two composers did not meet until 1827 when Beethoven was near death. However, in 1822 Schubert dedicated a set of piano variations to Beethoven, and with a published copy in hand went to greet the famous composer who was not at home. Uncomfortable by the idea of a return visit, Schubert simply left the edition. Beethoven apparently approved of the music and played it nearly every day for some time after.

—John Reed

PERFORMANCE NOTES

The Four Impromptus, D. 899 (Op. 90), belong to that rare breed of true masterpieces that enjoy enormous, enduring popularity among students, performers, and audiences alike. Having composed them in the fall of 1827, all four were sent by Schubert, apparently as a set, to the Viennese publisher Tobias Haslinger. Unfortunately, Haslinger published only the first two by December of that year. Impromptus Nos. 3 and 4 were not published until thirty years later by Tobias Haslinger's son Karl. The word "Impromptu" is written at the top of the first page of the manuscript in what may be the publisher's hand—not Schubert's—possibly to promote the piece among amateurs. It is quite conceivable, however, that Schubert approved of the title. He used it himself a few months later when he sent his second set of Four Impromptus, D. 935 (Op. 142), to the publisher Schott in Mainz.

By the time he composed the Impromptus (D. 899), Schubert had already written both large-scale piano works, such as sonatas and the "Wanderer Fantasy," and small-scale piano works, most notably several hundred dances. Similarly, he had written large-scale orchestral and chamber works, as well as hundreds of small-scale chamber works in his own unique genre, the lied (a song for solo voice and piano).

Schubert achieved a balance of form, style, and mood in the impromptus that often eluded him in his sonatas. That balance is apparent when each impromptu is played independently, and enhanced when performed as a complete set. Similarities between the four impromptus, and in particular between Nos. 2 and 4, are discussed below. However, despite these similarities each of the four has its own distinct character. Built upon a captivating melodic theme, No. 1 oscillates between lyricism and drama, struggle and resignation. No. 2 depicts extreme moods and is highly imaginative in its use of raw material, which consists mainly of diatonic and chromatic scales. The serene simplicity of the melody in No. 3 is set against a beautiful harmonic and textural backdrop. In No. 4, broken chords make up both the delicate sounds of part A and the contrasting melodic swells of part B, the Trio.

Most students are drawn to the variety of the impromptus' moods, the richness and beauty of their musical language, and their motivating technical challenges. From my own experience as a teacher I know that some students do well, even thrive, when presented with challenges. Inspired and motivated, they progress faster than they do without challenges. Others who shy away from serious challenges should first develop the basic skills necessary to tackle and benefit from the study of the impromptus.

There are enormous pedagogical and artistic benefits from playing the impromptus. Students will learn how to play repeated notes and chords, how to play fast passages evenly and lightly, how to produce a singing tone and shape a line, and how to voice chords. They will note the difference between legato, portato, and staccato playing; learn the careful use of the pedal; and explore subtle fluctuations in tempo. Perhaps most importantly, through the study of the impromptus, one becomes thoroughly conscious of the relevance and interconnection between the technical issues mentioned above and the musical, artistic challenges, a relationship that many études do not teach.

Each of the impromptus is long enough and challenging enough to qualify as an independent Romantic work for late-intermediate- and advanced-level students (and performers), and short enough to fit into various recital and competition programs. Unlike sonata movements, these can be presented in recitals singly, in any combination of two or three, or as a complete set. While they can be played and enjoyed by teenagers, their beauty, charm, inventiveness, and uniqueness tempt one to revisit them continually to discover hidden treasures.

The path to understanding Schubert's shorter piano works is through his lieder. The lieder show us how various emotions and ideas presented in the lied's text are translated by the composer into music. This includes how Schubert chooses to shape the melodic line; his choice of harmonic progressions, especially when using unusual, daring harmonies; and the role of the piano accompaniment in illustrating the text and its interaction with the vocal part. Studying the lieder is almost like having a dictionary defining Schubert's expressive musical language. In addition, the atmosphere, taste, and overall mood of Schubert's time and surroundings are reflected in the lieder and their texts, helping us understand him as a composer.

It is also important to listen to Schubert's chamber and orchestral music in order to be able to relate their sonorities and characteristics to the appropriate passages in Schubert's piano compositions. I provide specifics in the following discussion of each impromptu.

General Observations

Schubert and the Piano

"Schubert had but little technique…" wrote Ferdinand Hiller in an otherwise highly laudatory account of his first encounter with Schubert.[1] Hiller was not the only one to make this claim. Schubert was often depicted sitting at the piano during social/artistic gatherings. He produced numerous piano works, only few of which were written idiomatically for the instrument. In this music one can easily trace influences of the human voice, the string quartet or quintet, and the orchestra.

The performer's challenge is then two-fold: the artistic challenge of creating on the piano the sound of another instrument—or the illusion of the desired sound—including that of the human voice, and the technical challenge of applying techniques borrowed from other instruments to the piano. To effectively cope with this challenge, the performer should first listen to works that Schubert wrote for instruments other than the solo piano: lieder, string (or piano) trios/quartets/quintet, and symphonies.

Ironically, it is the piano's characteristic wide range, its rich tonal and harmonic potential, and its capacity to emulate sonorities of other instruments that allowed Schubert to write unidiomatic piano works.

Dynamics

The Viennese fortepiano had a much softer, more delicate tone than the modern piano. This is important to remember when playing *piano* and *pianissimo* passages. However, because of Schubert's familiarity with the sound of the full orchestra and that of Beethoven's piano works, I believe that Schubert's *fortissimo*—especially when paired with an exciting, passionate mood and full, rich texture—should be taken seriously. For example:

Impromptu No. 2 in E-flat Major, D. 899 (Op. 90): mm. 81–84

Fingering

I have included fingering where a certain, possibly unintuitive, fingering seems to work particularly well for me, or where the fingering that seems obvious from a technical point of view may not best serve the music. These are, of course, only suggestions as I recognize that each hand is different.

In a number of places I have redistributed notes between the two hands. These too are personal preferences noted where the musical meaning or expression might otherwise be compromised by my smallish hands. For example:

Impromptu No. 3 in G-flat Major, D. 899 (Op. 90): mm. 3–4

Analysis

Sheer pianism, without regard for the language of the composer and the building blocks of a musical work, results in a shallow and soulless interpretation; however, these Performance Notes do not include a note-by-note analysis. Whether harmonic, motivic, or structural, their purpose is to draw the performer's attention to some perhaps subtle compositional elements that directly affect the understanding and performance of the piece.

Tempo

The table below lists ranges of tempos which I believe are appropriate for these impromptus. The "correct" tempo depends on, and is an integral part of, many factors. These include tone, texture, articulation, dynamics, temperament, and mood. The below-listed tempo ranges take these factors as well as the composer's instructions into account. As with fingering, these are my suggestions. The final decision rests with the teacher or performer.

No. 1	♩ = 88–96 (mm. 1–40) ♩ = 96–104 (m. 41 onward)
No. 2	♩ = 180–200
No. 3	♩ = 66–80
No. 4	♩ = 138–144 ♩ = 134–144 (Trio)

Rhythm

There is a continuing debate over how to play a dotted-eighth-sixteenth figure against a triplet.

Some argue that in such case the dotted-eighth-sixteenth should always be treated as a triplet.

If we accept this argument, we assume by default that Schubert never intended this rhythmic combination as written.

I believe one has to decide on a case-by-case basis. Paul Badura-Skoda mentions Schubert's use of the following notation

in "Erstarung" from *Winterreise* (Winter's Journey). This interpretation is true, I believe, for this particular case. In other cases different interpretations may make sense.

In Impromptu No. 1, it is quite obvious that the dotted rhythm must not be changed into a triplet. Triplets are not introduced until m. 41, by which time the rhythmic, marchlike character of the theme is well-established.

Another example is from the finale of the Sonata in B-flat Major, D. 960. (Please refer to the discussion on Impromptu No. 1 for similarities between these two pieces.) The dancelike first theme and accompaniment of this rondo–sonata movement consist of eighth notes.

Sonata in B-flat Major, D. 960: mm. 1–5

In mm. 215–224, the opening measure of this theme with the upbeat shortened to a sixteenth note is presented over triplets; the triplets echoing mm. 185–215.

Sonata in B-flat Major, D. 960: mm. 215–218

Is the theme's upbeat to be played as part of a triplet? I don't think it should as it would not be in line with its character.

In the 1827 Haslinger Edition of Impromptu No. 1 (which I think should be "taken with a grain of salt," see Sources, Articulation, and discussion of Impromptu No. 1), the sixteenth note is always lined up with the last note of the triplet, while in m. 68 the B-flat eighth note is placed right between the second and third notes of the triplet.

Impromptu No. 1 in C minor, D. 899 (Op. 90),
1827 Haslinger Edition: m. 68

Impromptu No. 1 in C minor, D. 899 (Op. 90),
Bärenreiter Edition: mm. 56–57, 80–81

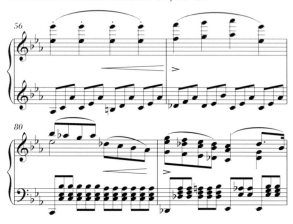

In this particular example, the manuscript is not helpful as Schubert rarely lines up the right- and left-hand parts, and often uses shorthand to indicate triplets ♪. and sextuplets ♩..

Ornamentation

There are several questions regarding the performance of appoggiaturas. Are they to be played on the beat or as grace notes before it? How long or short should they be? Does the presence of a stroke across the stem make a difference?

In his edition of Schubert's shorter works for piano, Paul Badura-Skoda writes: "In his songs, Schubert often writes long appoggiaturas in the vocal part, but he always writes out the same appoggiaturas in large notes in the piano part. This means that appoggiaturas in Schubert's piano music (and his music for other instruments) are to be played short as a matter of principle."[2] Supposing we accept this, we still have to decide whether to play them on or before the beat. In the 1827 edition of No. 1 (see Sources), all appoggiaturas are printed as eighth notes with a slash (cross-stroke) across the stem, in contrast with the manuscript in which they are written as sixteenth notes without a slash.

Interpretation of these ornaments depends on the shape and flow of the ornamented line and on the harmony. My own choices can be heard on the companion recordings. I leave this open to the performer as I believe that either possibility may be stylistically and aesthetically justified.

Accents

It is easy to be confused by what appear to be accents in some editions of Impromptu No. 1.

In other editions (including this one), these markings are indicated as diminuendo hairpins. Some editors reason that this is due to Schubert's handwriting, which makes the hairpin look too short to be a decrescendo or diminuendo, and therefore look like an accent.

The manuscript provides what I believe is the answer to the above dilemma. Schubert, writing with a feather, made horizontal lines from left to right. The crescendo hairpin consists of two such lines, each written left to right. By contrast, the decrescendo hairpin was written in one stroke, left to right, with a short return to the left. The result is an overall shorter hairpin than the crescendo that was written in two strokes. When compared solely with crescendo signs, the decrescendo may appear to be an accent mark. However, careful examination of the manuscript and the musical context leaves little doubt (in most cases) as to which is an accent and which a decrescendo.

As with many accents, we still must decide whether it is agogic (a stress created by extended duration), or whether we must play louder or more *espressivo*.

Pedal

Aside from the general "[col] pedale" at the beginning of No. 3, Schubert provided no pedal markings. (In all of Schubert's piano music there are only a few pedal markings.) I have indicated limited pedaling suggestions only in Impromptu No. 3.

Articulation

It is not always clear from the manuscript where a slur starts and where it ends. Moreover, some of the clearer notations are not always consistent with other apparently clear notations. The 1827 edition of No. 1 is not helpful either because of inconsistencies both with the manuscript and within the edition itself.

So in the case of slurs, we have to make decisions using our understanding of the specific music and our knowledge of Schubert's style in addition to all available sources.

Sources

I was fortunate to have had the opportunity to carefully examine the autograph manuscript of all four impromptus and the first edition of Impromptu No. 1 (published in 1827 by Tobias Haslinger), now held in the Pierpont Morgan Library, New York City. As this edition appeared during Schubert's lifetime, it is less likely to deviate from Schubert's intentions. (The substantial editorial changes in the 1857 edition of No. 3 prove this point. See discussion of Impromptu No. 3.) Unlike Beethoven, however, Schubert did not have much control over details and proofs of his works' editions. We cannot assume that inconsistencies between the manuscript and the first edition are necessarily Schubert's last moment revisions. After carefully examining the two above-mentioned invaluable sources I chose the version that, to the best of my knowledge and understanding, seemed the most consistent with Schubert's intentions and style.

I found the combination of scholarly work and artistic common sense in Paul Badura-Skoda's work for the Wiener Urtext Edition helpful and inspiring. This edition also contains the first draft of Impromptu No. 1, giving us a glimpse into Schubert's creative process. I have also consulted the Henle, Bärenreiter, and the Breitkopf & Härtel editions.

Notes on the Impromptus

Impromptu No. 1 in C minor, D. 899 (Op. 90)
Epic in style and content, this is the most complex and most challenging of the four. It is, I believe, Schubert in a nutshell. It is lyrical with occasional outbursts and mood swings; it references lieder and other works; it demonstrates the Romantic sense of wandering; it alludes to Beethoven; and it employs chamber and orchestral techniques and sonorities.

The opening—*fortissimo* double octave Gs sustained by the fermata—sets the stage for a poetic, lyrical, and exciting balladelike piece. The finale of the Sonata in B-flat Major, D. 960, which was completed about a year later, has much in common with this impromptu (and interestingly with the finale of Beethoven's String Quartet, Op. 130). Both start on a loud G octave and are

followed by a theme built around B-natural–C–D, containing repeated notes. Written in Beethoven's dramatic key of C minor and opening with a somber theme, this impromptu may or may not have been influenced by Beethoven's death only a few months earlier. (Schubert had visited Beethoven only one week before the latter's death. That was the first and last time the two men, who lived in the same city, met.) Nevertheless, it does contain Beethovenian elements of struggle, side by side with typically Schubertian lyrical elements.

The rhythmic opening theme—a walking-pace "journey theme" typical of the ones throughout *Winterreise*—is transformed into a lyrical, poetic theme in A-flat major, accompanied by flowing triplets (m. 41). This accompaniment becomes agitated and chordal in m. 74, as it alternates with the melody between the two hands. Here we encounter Schubert's use of technical elements borrowed from other instruments. The accompaniment, not unlike the piano part in *Erlkönig*, is evocative of a tremolo on string instruments.

In the following fifty measures the dynamics shift back and forth between *pianissimo* and *forte* or *fortissimo* no fewer than nine times. These extreme changes are striking. One may think of a ballade in which the hero, represented by the melodic theme, has various experiences and various emotions.

A short lull in the repeated triplets introduces a new texture, with a pizzicatolike bass and arabesque-style, broken chords accompanying the melodic theme. This is strikingly similar to the second theme group in the aforementioned finale of the B-flat major sonata.

When the piece returns to its tonality of C, it is in the major mode, but the feeling is that of resignation, not one of hope.

Persistent, relentless Gs carry the "message" of the opening octaves throughout the entire piece to its end, where soft G octaves are distant memories of the *fortissimo* opening.

Technically, the repeated notes and chords are the most challenging. They must be even in sound and timing, and never overpower the melodic line. Staying close to the keys and working with the keys' own action within a small range of motion make it easier to repeat notes and to control the tone.

The wide dynamic range, rich colors, and variety of touches of this impromptu lend themselves well to orchestration. Imagining the colors and timbres of the various orchestral instruments helps characterize the different sections of the piece.

A major artistic challenge is keeping the piece together while allowing slight fluctuations in tempo.

Impromptu No. 2 in E-flat Major, D. 899 (Op. 90)
The fast runs and extensive use of the upper, brilliant register of the piano indicate a strong influence by pianist-composers such as Hummel and Clementi.[3]

The form is A–B–A plus Coda.

The subtle syncopation in the left-hand accompaniment of part A matures into a real syncopation, emphasized by a chord and an accent in part B. Where and how this transition occurs is interesting and consequential. In mm. 71–76, Schubert places *forzando* signs on the first beat of each measure. Then in mm. 77–79, the *forzando* moves to the second beat. In the editions I have examined, the *forzandos* in mm. 77–79 are written above the right-hand part, implying that the right-hand note (or perhaps both hands) is to be accentuated. However, the manuscript tells a somewhat different story. Schubert writes the *forzando* signs below the left-hand staff (despite this area of the staff being crowded and despite having ample room above the right-hand part), indicating that the *forzando* was meant for the left-hand chord. In other words, the above-mentioned transition takes place right here, before and in anticipation of part B.

The small, upward leap before the descent softens the downbeat and lends an expressive touch to the scale work.

mm. 1 and 6

It helps to imagine that the scale figures start on the highest note and to practice them that way. To balance this, performers should play the upward leap legato. (Note Schubert's indication of "legato" at the very opening of the piece.) Studying works by Hummel and Clementi before learning this impromptu may assist with its technical aspects.

Written in the minor mode of the lowered sub-mediant (the Neapolitan relation favored by Schubert), part B (the Trio) is rhythmic, syncopated, and marked *fortissimo* and *ben marcato*, with an abundance of accent signs and *forzando*— and stands in stark contrast with the mostly soft and flowing part A. I believe Schubert meant what he wrote here, and therefore I suggest taking all accents, *fortissimos*, etc., at face value.

This trio offers a glimpse of a lesser-known side of Schubert's character, described by his friends as follows:

> Anyone who knew Schubert knows how he was made of two natures, foreign to each other…
> —Josef Kenner, a childhood friend

> …in Schubert there slumbered a dual nature.
> —Eduard von Bauernfeld, a dramatist who knew Schubert well in his last years

> As soon as the blood of the vine was glowing in him, he liked to withdraw into a corner and give in to a quiet, comfortable anger during which he would try to create some sort of havoc as quickly as possible, for example, with cups, glasses and plates, and as he did so, he would grin and screw up his eyes tight.
> —Wilhelm von Chezy, author and journalist[4]

It should be noted that the idea of two natures in one body was common in nineteenth-century Europe. It was a manifestation of, among other things, beauty born out of sorrow— the image of the suffering artist.

In light of the above, it is easier to make sense of the Coda. Based on the trio, Schubert further emphasizes this music's excited— indeed, impatient—character by introducing an accelerando towards the end of the piece.

Impromptu No. 3 in G-flat Major, D. 899 (Op. 90)
It should come as no surprise that the composer of some 600 lieder wrote beautiful, captivating melodic lines not only for voice but also for instruments. This impromptu can qualify as a "Song Without Words," a lied in which the piano plays both the melody and the accompaniment.

The choice of key is remarkable, with six flats and an extensive use of black keys throughout the piece. This was new, daring, and visionary.

In the Classical era, composers seldom wrote in tonalities with more than four accidentals. One noteworthy exception was Beethoven, who in 1809 chose to write his Sonata No. 24, Op. 78, in the then unusual key of F-sharp major. However, Beethoven, who enjoyed in his lifetime the popularity and status Schubert never even approached, could afford to stay his ground, although a key with six accidentals would have been certain to scare away potential buyers (and publishers).

Tonalities with many accidentals and many black keys only became popular later in the Romantic era. Interestingly, Schubert had already used such black-key tonalities in several of his dances and was to again use the key of G-flat for the first of his Three Piano Pieces, D. 946, composed some seven months later.

Also noteworthy is the time signature 4/2, indicated by two cut-time signs placed next to each other. That the time and key signatures were at least somewhat unusual is evident by the fact that in 1857—a full thirty years after its composition—the publisher changed the key to G major and the meter to the familiar 2/2. This was no doubt in order to promote sales by making the piece more appealing, less complicated, and less threatening to potential buyers. (The changes were made on the manuscript and are clearly evident.) But by doing so, the publisher Karl Haslinger missed some of the more unique, important, and subtle points of the piece.

The tonality of G major is wrong on several counts. All four impromptus are written in keys with flats, as are the Four Impromptus, D. 935 (Op. 142), composed at about the same time. A piece with a sharp (G major) appears out of place. Technically, playing this piece on mainly black keys is easier than playing it on mainly white ones. The hand sits better and enjoys more flexibility on the black keys. The darker color of G-flat major better suits the mood of piece.

Haslinger's change of meter undermines the very nature of the piece. Composers often find fascinating and original ways in which to use the limited (and limiting) language of musical notation to express ideas and intentions. Beethoven's original meters in the slow movement of Sonata Opus 111 come to mind. Though not on this scale of originality, the impromptu's unusual meter conveys an essential part of its character. The 4/2 meter feels broad and expansive, allowing for long phrases. The half-note beats are slow enough for the music to not feel rushed.

A lied for the piano, the impromptu's texture consists of three layers: a melodic line on top, a bass line at the bottom, and broken chords in the center—similar to many of Schubert's songs such as "Wohin?" from *Die schöne Müllerin* and "Liebesbotschaft" from *Schwanengesang*.

The above points highlight two important characteristics of this impromptu. The top line must be nicely shaped and, despite the *pianissimo*, should sing. The performer should ensure that the triplets/sextuplets of the accompaniment are even, but never static, never mechanical. They too must flow and be beautifully shaped. Practicing the piece without the top line is helpful.

When first learning the piece, a small physical adjustment goes a long way. By moving the music to the left part of the music rack, the pianist can look straight ahead when playing this piece, which is written mostly for the center and left part of the keyboard.

Impromptu No. 4 in A-flat Major, D. 899 (Op. 90)
As noted in the comments to No. 2, these two impromptus share a number of characteristics. Structurally, both are in A–B–A form (No. 2 also has a Coda). Uncharacteristic for Schubert, both are pianistic, employing fast, light runs and extensive use of the upper, brilliant register of the piano. Both are in 3/4 meter and share a gently syncopated second beat in the left-hand part. While No. 2 consists mainly of scale work, No. 4 consists of an arabesquelike form of broken chords.

The syncopated motive is present throughout the impromptu; but because of the often subtle way in which it is presented, it may not always be obvious. It first appears in the left-hand accompaniment as a long note (chord) on the second beat. Then in mm. 23, 25 and 27, the highest and loudest notes of the chord progressions fall on the second beat, followed by descending steps that diminuendo.

A new, melodic theme introduced in m. 47 in the tenor is marked throughout by expressive accents and long notes on the second beat. All of the above, as well as the melodic right-hand motive in mm. 72–73 and 76–77, have in common a rise in pitch from the first to the second beat. In fact, the broken chord figure of the right-hand sixteenths is marked by a small upward leap from the first to the second note, similar to the right-hand figures of No. 2. This expressive leap is more pronounced in the Trio (part B). In mm. 115, 117, 125, 129, etc., this leap helps shape the crescendo and moves the line forward. A descending step with emphasis on the first beat (mm. 157–158) reverses the process towards the Trio's conclusion.

Awareness of this motivic unity is vital for a meaningful performance. While each of the different themes and moods must be clearly characterized, this unifying element, present throughout the piece, must not be ignored.

To prevent the sixteenths from sounding mechanical, the performer should use ever-so-subtle fluctuations of speed. For example, the performer could slow down the first or last few notes as if speaking them.

—*Immanuela Gruenberg*

Notes:

1. McKay, *Franz Schubert: A Biography*, p. 276.
2. Badura-Skoda, ed., *Schubert: Impromptus, Moments musicaux, Drei Klavierstücke*, p. vi.
3. Schubert met Hummel in Vienna in March 1827, when Schubert was thirty years old and Hummel forty-nine. Hummel "was so deeply moved that tears trickled down his cheeks" in response to Schubert's music. The following year Schubert dedicated his last three piano sonatas to Hummel. (McKay, *Franz Schubert: A Biography*, p. 276.)
4. These three quotations are all from McKay, *Franz Schubert: A Biography*, p. 134, 135, and 147, respectively.

References

Sources and Suggested Reading:

Blume, Friedrich. *Classic and Romantic Music*, trans. M. D. Herter Norton. New York: W. W. Norton, 1970.

Brown, Maurice J. E. *Essays on Schubert*. London: Macmillan, 1966.

_____. *Schubert: A Critical Biography*. New York: St. Martin's Press, 1966.

_____. "Schubert, Franz (Peter)," *The New Grove Dictionary of Music and Musicians*, 20 vols., ed. Stanley Sadie. London: Macmillan, 1980, XVI, 752–811.

Dahlhaus, Carl. *Nineteenth-Century Music*, trans. Bradford Robinson. Berkeley, Los Angeles: University of California Press, 1989.

Deutsch, Otto Erich. *Franz Schubert: Briefe und Schriften*. Wien: Hellinek, 1954.

_____. *The Schubert: Thematic Catalogue*. New York: Dover Publications, Inc., 1995.

Frisch, Walter, ed. *Schubert: Critical and Analytical Studies*. Lincoln: University of Nebraska Press, 1986.

Griffel, L. Michael. "The Romantic and Post Romantic Eras," *Schirmer History of Music*. New York: Schirmer Books, 1982.

McKay, Elizabeth Norman. *Franz Schubert: a Biography*. New York: Oxford University Press, 1996.

Plantinga, Leon. *Romantic Music*, New York: W. W. Norton, 1984.

Rosen, Charles. *The Romantic Generation*. Cambridge: Harvard University Press, 1995.

Rosenblum, Sandra P. *Performance Practice in Classic Piano Music*. Bloomington and Indianapolis: Indiana University Press, 1988.

Scores:

Badura-Skoda, Paul, ed. *Schubert: Impromptus, Moments musicaux, Drei Klavierstücke*. Vienna: Wiener Urtext Edition, 1973 (1969).

Breitkopf and Härtel Critical Edition of 1884–1897. *Schubert: Complete Works*. New York: Dover Publications, Inc., 1969.

Gieseking, Walter, ed. *Schubert: Impromptus Op. 90, D. 899*. Munich: G. Henle Verlag, 1974.

Landon, Christa, ed. *Schubert: Impromptus, D. 899*. Kassel: Bärenreiter, 2003.

Schubert, Franz. *Four Impromptus*. Manuscript, 1827.

_____. *Impromptu in C Minor, Op. 90*. Vienna: Tobias Haslinger, 1827.

Acknowledgement

A special note of thanks to the Pierpont Morgan Library in New York, and especially to the very helpful staff of their Reading Room, for letting me examine the manuscript and the first edition of No. 1. The latter was brought in expressly for my use.

Impromptu No. 1 in C minor

Franz Schubert
D. 899 (Op. 90)

Allegro molto moderato

* The suggested fingering allows for legato of the alto part. The alternate fingering enables legato of top part.

**In the manuscript, Schubert grouped beats 1 and 2 under one slur, and 3 and 4 under another. Such slurs are inconsistent with similar passages (mm. 2, 10, etc.) but echo the two-note motive of this piece (mm. 90, 163, 176), blending, perhaps subconsciously, the two motives.

Impromptu No. 2 in E-flat Major

Franz Schubert
D. 899 (Op. 90)

* Although untraditional, this fingering makes for smoother, more even playing.

*alternate hand distribution:

Impromptu No. 3 in G-flat Major

Franz Schubert
D. 899 (Op. 90)

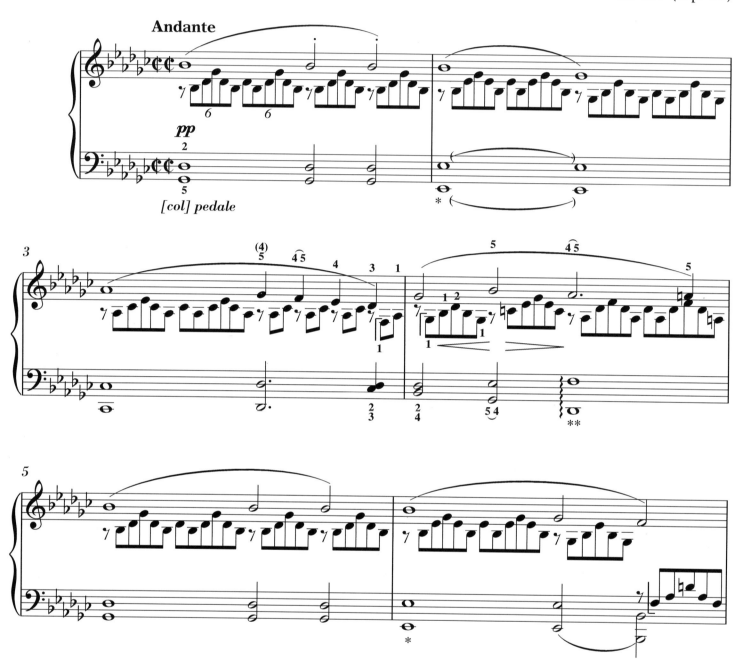

* In many editions the bass notes in these measures are connected by ties. These are similar to the ties in mm. 8 and 20 and correspond to mm. 56, 62, and 66. They do not appear in the manuscript, however. Since the recapitulation differs from the opening in other ways, I prefer to follow the manuscript. Small changes between the opening and recapitulation add interest.

*See footnote on first page.

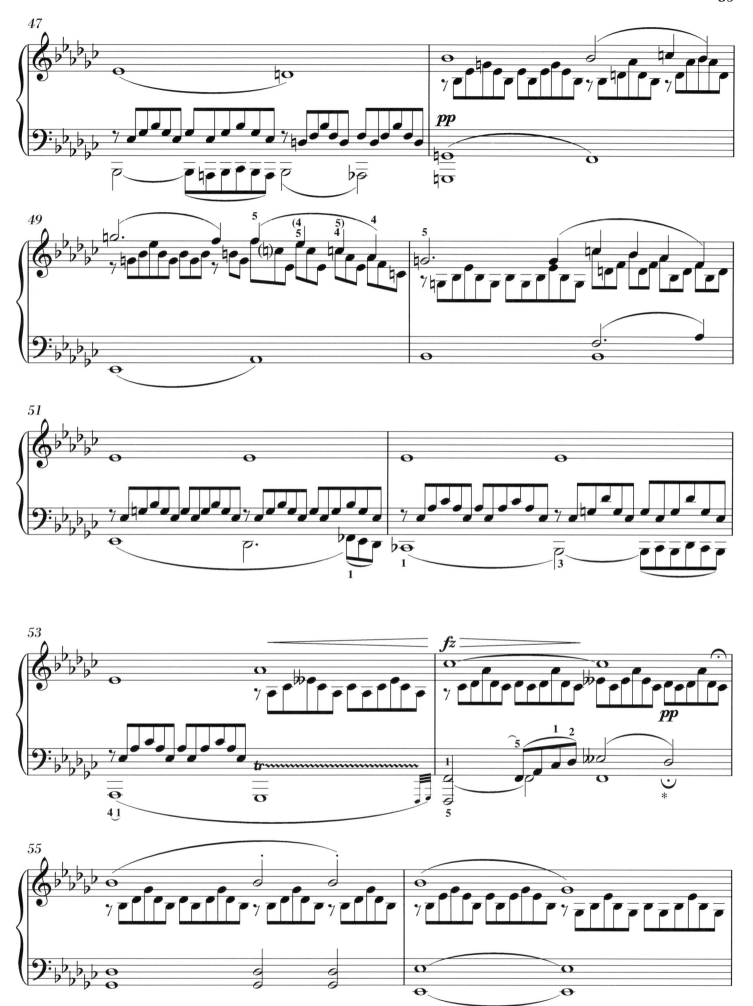

* In the manuscript, Schubert places one large fermata above the last four notes of the bar. We have replaced this
  with a more standard notation.

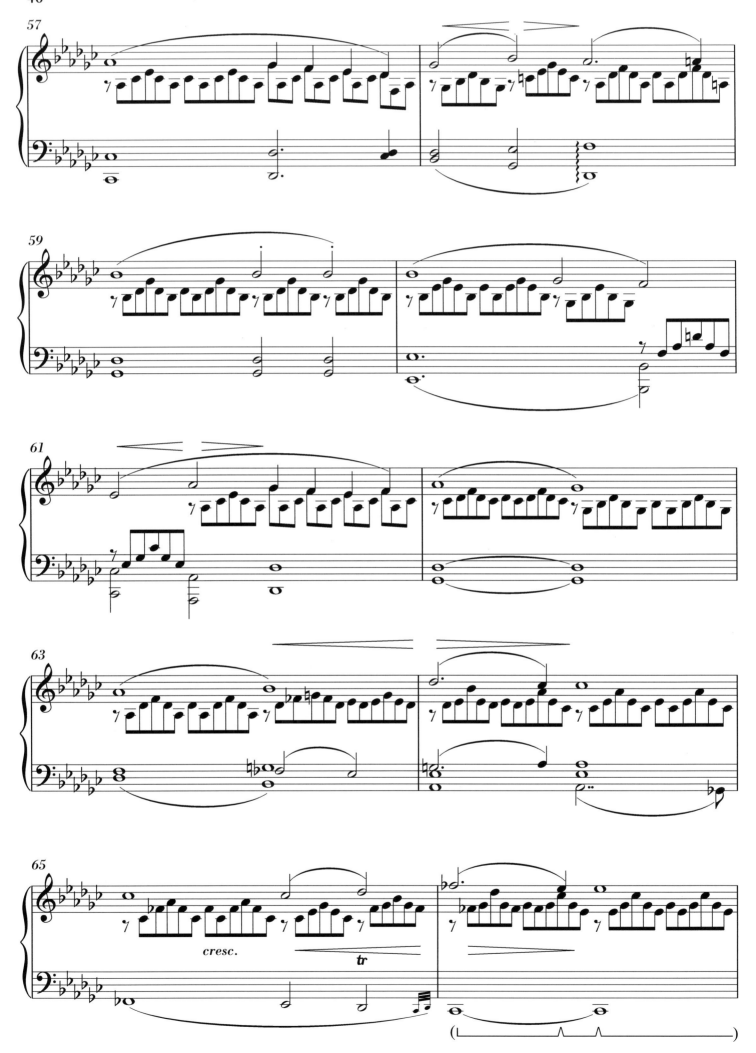

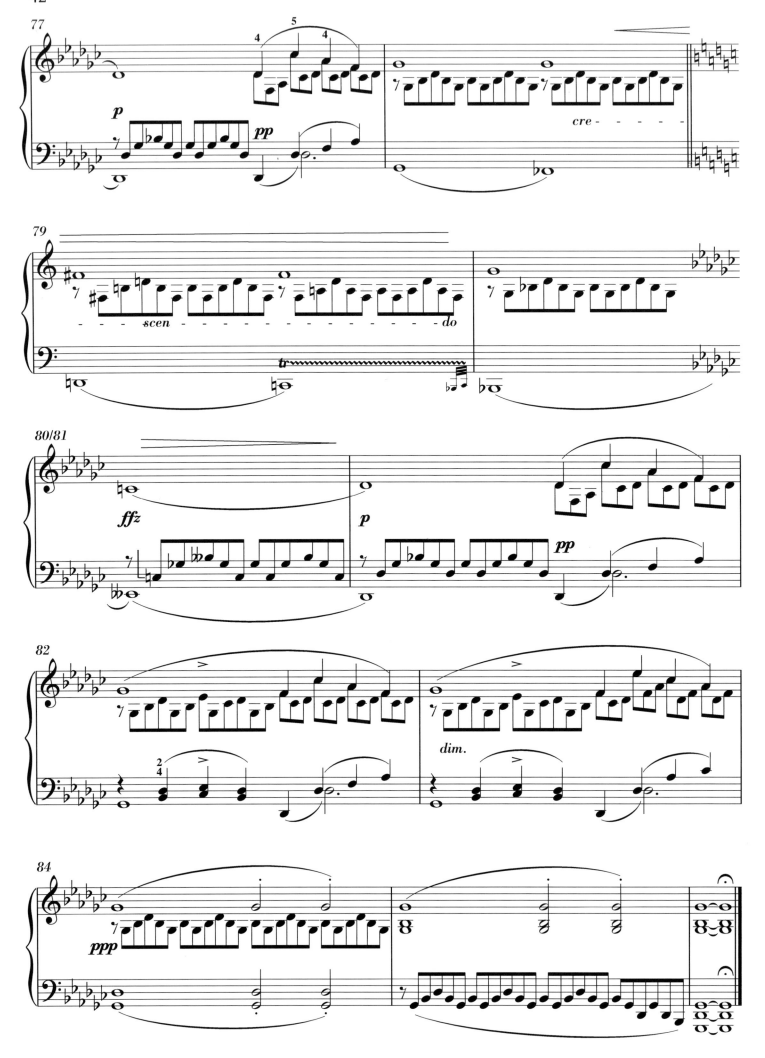

Impromptu No. 4 in A-flat Major

Franz Schubert
D. 899 (Op. 90)

* Finger-pedal the bass while changing the pedal for a clean melodic line:

ABOUT THE EDITOR

IMMANUELA GRUENBERG

Immanuela Gruenberg is an active recitalist, chamber musician, lecturer, teacher, and competition adjudicator. She has given concerts, lectures, master classes, and conducted workshops on piano performance, literature, and pedagogy in the United States, South America, Israel, and the Far East. Critics have praised her playing as "supreme artistry" (*Richmond News Leader*), "lyrical and dramatic" (*Buenos Aires Herald*), and "delicate sonorities" (*Haaretz*, Tel Aviv); her writing as "highly intelligent" (*Richmond News Leader*); and her research as "scholarly" and "so well thought out." She has been commended for programs of "unusual interest," for having "spoke[n] intelligently about each piece" (*The Washington Post*), and for lectures that "exceeded our highest expectations" (*MSMTA Convention Newsletter*).

She began her musical career in her native Israel, performing as soloist and as a member of the Tel Aviv Trio, in venues including the Israel Museum in Jerusalem, the Tel Aviv Museum of Art, and the Chamber Music Series of the Israel Philharmonic Orchestra. She recorded for and was heard on Kol HaMusica, Israel's classical radio station. In the United States she has appeared on stages including the Kennedy Center, the Corcoran Gallery, and the Strathmore Mansion. She performed at the Smithsonian Institution's "Piano 300" series, celebrating the 300th anniversary of the invention of the piano; presented lecture recitals in the United States and in Tel Aviv in honor of Schubert's 200th birthday; and performed Josef Tal's Concerto for Piano and Electronics in Jerusalem in honor of Tal's 85th birthday.

A magna cum laude graduate of the Rubin Academy of Music of the Tel Aviv University and a thirteen-time winner of the America Israel Cultural Foundation scholarship, Dr. Gruenberg is the recipient of numerous prizes and awards. As a scholarship student at the Manhattan School of Music, she completed the Doctor of Musical Arts degree in only two years. She studied piano with Arie Vardi and Constance Keene, and chamber music with Boris Berman and Rami Shevelov. She also coached with Thomas Schumacher and Zitta Zohar.

Dr. Gruenberg was a teaching assistant at the Manhattan School of Music in New York, and a faculty member of the Music Teachers' College in Tel Aviv and the Levine School of Music in Washington, D. C. She maintains a private studio in Potomac, Maryland, and is currently chair of the Washington International Competition.